Jerome Prairie Creation Myths
and other Farm Tales

Jerome Prairie Creation Myths and other Farm Tales

poems

Lisa E Baldwin

N8tive Run Press

Jerome Prairie, Oregon

First Printing

ISBN 979-8-9866994-1-7

Published by N8tive Run Press
ৡৡ৻(৵৵৶

N8tive Run Press
  — a subsidiary of N8tive Run Enterprises
5007 Laurel Avenue
Grants Pass, Oregon 97527

n8tiverun.enterprises@gmail.com

front cover photo: *Pi Day 2018*, L.E. Baldwin
author photo by Cynthia Spear

Dedication

For Jack,

my patient and kind partner in life;

For Kate,

my dear friend through thick and thin;

And for Nick,

my amazing and beautiful son.

Contents

Jerome Prairie Creation Myths and other Farm Tales

I

Jerome Prairie Creation Myths

Why Butterflies Fly

Long time ago, long time,
a curious young grub came up
into spring-warmed grass
and dreamed of living
in the light
under the blue sky above.
She longed to be closer,
so she began to climb
upward toward the sky,
up the root-rise of the big maple.
It took a long time,
many years and generations,
and the dream continued.
Up, up, into the canopy
of tender green new leaf
where the breeze in the leaves
feels like flying.
Having learned from the maple
the value of bark and a winter sleep,
from the neighboring spiders
the skill of spinning,
she fattened up for the longest winter,
wrapped from top to bottom
in a silky cocoon, and the dream continued
into a springtime so full
of blossom and shine,
the colors and light seeped through
the cocoon walls and painted her
in beauty, gave her wings to fly.
Butterflies fly because
long time ago, long time,
she wanted to.

What I Know

I don't know about
the world at large.
I know about country
things, here-on-the-farm things.
The butternut squash is vining and blossoming.
All the cultivated berries are nearly done
just as the wild blackberries are coming on
with the heaviest fruit set in years.
Pears, too. The sparrows in the trees and boxes
are feeding second-clutch chicks.
The beehives are humming long hours,
these warm honey days of July.
And soon, likely tomorrow or the next
tomorrow, the farm and garden
will fill with the first flights
of midsummer butterflies, new
in the world at large.

Frog Song

—translated from the original Pseudacris regilla

Come on   Come on
I sing for you my love
Am strong for you this song
for you I sing.

I fill the air   I fill the night
I am I am I am for you
your mate   your mate
your song I sing our song:

I am the one for you,
My song the one to find.
Tune out the common chord.
Come on, tonight, come on
tonight
                tonight

to-night.

Farm Work

The earthworm plows the ground,
Feeds the roots.
The birds and wind plant the seed.
Trees provide the mulch,
Clouds bring the water.
Bees play matchmaker,
With the buzz and Barry White.
The sun, once risen, is Boss.

But come sundown and night-shade
When the stars unfade to shine,
A magic mist lifts out of the fields
And dresses the farm in diamonds,
Dewdrops and party lights—
    They catch the moon
    Make the nighthawks croon
    And dung-beetles swoon
    Working the night-shift in June.

Crickets

They come on, the opening act,
with a song so clear,
a voice so pure
it is the metaphor for silence,
the absence of voice, the sound of silence.

The farm is momentarily mute.

Then the call to harmony rises,
rises as a choral fugue,
awakens the frogs,
brings the raccoons to the pond to wash up,
stirs the owl to wing.

Bird Lessons
> **to my future grandchildren**

Pay attention to all the birds,
the teachers here on the farm
which may or may not be the center
of the Bird World. If you can learn
the lessons they carry in
on winged deliveries, and learn
their patterns, seasonal and otherwise,
you will know much more about how to be
and survive in the peopled world.

Red-headed woodpeckers teach
persistence, the value of hard work,
smart work, with their tap-tap-tap…
listen…move…tap-tap-listen.
They waste no time, take few breaks,
and keep their families fed.

Golden eagles and red-shouldered hawks
exemplify the virtue of being well-informed,
alert, interested, aware and wary.
They know all that happens here
on the farm and all the fields around,
They spread the news, town criers in the sky.
When they call, look up. Listen up. Look up.

Canada Geese are the taskmasters of practicality,
getting their chores done while venting their stress
as they move from dampness to dampness,
being useful cartographers for irrigation season.

The Mallards, Brently and Louise, will drop in
fairly often to feed on the pond, and sometimes
they'll linger longer after heads-down, tails-up,
gliding leisurely around, showing
how easy it is to find peace on the farm.
Ducks on calm water are harbingers
of good days to come. They bring us hope.

For indelible beauty, a necessity for survival,
few sights surpass the unexpected flight
of the ring-necked pheasant sailing low
on steadfast wings, just skimming over
the tall grass ripening in the field.

How the Sky was Filled with Wings

In the same way that
Hope, when it comes,
Pulls your shoulders up
— draws your spine to length—
Turns your eyes skyward,

How in the early times,
In the beginning times,
Some wisp of new-formed life,
Some tendril of wind-waved hope
In upward longing

Was lifted to flight,
—Lifted to wing—
On warm rising air
And forever married
Earth and Sky.

Kettle of Eagles over Jerome Prairie

To be one of you, soaring high.
To see as you see, from above,
looking down not up on
The Siskiyous in winter,
snow-covered heads and wrinkled faces,
dark bodies below.

And in spring, can you see the wind
colored white by a flurry
of pear blossoms, swirling
and rising as wishes,
as promises made and kept?

Are you one in a kettle of eagles,
uplifted higher by thermodynamics?
Do you view the green circles of summer
in fields with mechanized water
as a polka-dot tapestry or some
whimsical art installation for raptors?

When the slant of light tilts
toward autumn and days grow short,
do you follow the routes of three rivers,
curving along banks of yellowed maples
brightly trimming blue-green hills
braided with bronzed oaks?

I see you aloft, flying high and away,
and long to go with you,
to see the world as you see it,
as I, Earth-bound, can only imagine.

The Muse of Gardening

She makes a delicate entrance,
pastel and sweet daphne,
petite and polite crocus.
The party doesn't get boisterous
until all the guests have arrived:
tulips in full bloom bring a riot of color;
hyacinths perfume the air all around;
daffodils pop up like laughter from the earth,
heads nodding atop their slender necks
as if to say, *Oh my, yes! That's a good one!*
The seasonal cotillion rolls on through the cycle.
Mature leaves of summer shade and shelter,
and put the youngsters to bed.
Long still days and calm starry nights
carry on, uninterrupted, with few exceptions—
an August cloudburst, a rumble of thunder—
but gradually, the evening air grows cooler,
cooler still then cold. And once again
color comes on subtly at first, then roars
and rends the sky, raises the roof,
flashy as lit neon, glowing and golden,
deep reds and burnished bronze.
It's a farewell, a retirement party,
and thanks for all the good work.
The cycle will come full around,
and winter— dressed in grays and silver,
shrouded night skies, moonless and starless—
pays respects, graveside: a heavy rain
drums a death march, plays a dirge,
quenches thirsty roots and bulbs
that will wake and rise again.

What Comes Up Must Go Down

Making a living on the land is hard
soft as we have become

A bluebird day in mid-spring
swells pear blossoms open

Just ahead of a killing frost
on a wildly starry night

Morning sun warms damp ground
luring the most anxious seeds to push

Tender sweet peas sprout up
into the light to feed themselves

By afternoon, the late-spring sun
withers new green back into loose soil

I've heard the roots of a mature maple
mirror underground the tree above

As the highest branches reach new heights
roots grow deeper and more complex

Nature's Library

These leaves belong to the land.
These leaves have listened to the land.
The land is full of stories
no other listener has heard ,
like pages in an unread book,
a true collection of leaves.
The trees collect the stories
from the land and the sky
and hold them, reserved
in the rings and seasons under bark,
rustled by the wind
the leaves tell stories
in lullaby tones,
too soft to hear
without really listening.

Late Summer Field Guide

Now August arrives—
Canada geese flock in fields
before the Fall flight

From the field's far edge
the sound of water running—
wind in cottonwoods

A richness of blue
above these vast fields of green—
Red-tail has domain

Second cut of hay—
timothy, rye and clover—
horses' winter feed

Shadow of an owl
cast in waxing half-moon light
stirs a young field mouse

Summer to Autumn must yield—
flock, wind, hawk, hay, mouse and field

Holy Solstice

Trees shoo the night clouds
and open a dark window
lit by bright starlight.

The Great Conjunction—
high above the swaying trees
two planets unite.

Awash in stardust
the frosted trees, ever green,
bathe in rarest light.

It will shine again
in a winter far beyond
our lives here on Earth.

What eyes will then turn?
What hearts ache for Bethlehem
and trees under stars?

From one tree three owls take flight
on this brightest holy night.

Note about Form: *Holy Solstice* and the previous poem, *Late Summer Field Guide* are both Corona Haiku, or a Crown of Haiku (derived from a Crown of Sonnets), a new poetic form I invented in 2021. The structure imposed here is a sequence of five stanzas in haiku form plus an ending couplet, totaling seventeen lines long overall (to echo the 17 syllables in one haiku). A recurring image links the sections of the poem, a nod to the the origins of haiku in the renga, another Japanese form. The two lines in the couplet must rhyme and must be 7 syllables each in length to create coherence with the haiku's middle line. Also the 14 syllable count in the couplet echoes the 14-line structure of sonnets, the most recognized form to employ an ending couplet. I know I have completely unleashed my inner poetry geek with all this, but I kind of like it.—LEB

Owl Night

On silent wings the owl takes flight
In a moonless sky, alone
Over these fields, snowbound and white.

The stillness of a late winter night
Shines a beauty all its own.
On silent wings, the owl takes flight.

The hunter sees in scant starlight
Skittish sign of fur and bone
Moving in fields, snowbound and white.

Instinct and hunger and essence ignite
A dive with no shadow thrown.
On silent wings the owl takes flight.

Noiseless descent from transcendent height
At speeds with power unknown
Down to these fields, snowbound and white.

The hunter, the hunt—a natural rite
And the brilliance of stars is outshone.
On silent wings, the owl takes flight,
Sailing these fields, snowbound and white.

A (superlative) Winter Carol

The shortest days of December
leave the fewest hours for grieving,
give the longest hours to dream.
These deepest nights of winter are
perhaps most beautiful without a moon,
with a new moon or just the slimmest crescent
in the clearest, blackest heavens
when the lights of our passed loves
fill the darkest sky. Perhaps
the greatest beauty is the cloistered
silence in a clouded winter night,
the sound of falling
snow on fallen snow, whitest Earth
aglow in the dark. Then again
perhaps there is no beauty
finer than the fullest moon, light
shining on fields of drifted snow,
and the quietest world, so hushed
only the most tender memories echo,
the most sacred carols are sung.

Truths of October

The winter squash are gathered.
Washed, dried, stored,
They are vessels of optimism
Set aside for the dark days
That will most certainly come.
The season turns in swirls
Of yellow and crimson leaf flurry whirls
As the world clears away
Summer's clutter; a gaudy abundance
Gives way to simple truths:
    Golden sunlight can be kept
    In butternut flesh;
    The fully ripened life
    Has the richest hues;
    And Time in transition is beautiful.

Watch for Falling Rock

On a trip down the Smith River highway
Shortly after I learned to read
I asked about the sign.
My father told the story
Of a young boy who wandered
Away from his home and was lost.
His father searched for him.
His whole tribe searched for him.
They called his name,
Echoed it up the draws,
Down the river canyon,
Over the mud flats,
Through the big timber,
And still the boy was lost.
Years passed and the father aged.
No longer able to walk the hills
And unable to stop searching,
Afraid his son would think
He had been forgotten, forsaken,
The old man with help
From the scattering tribe
Put signs in all the places
His son loved best
To let him know forever
He was missed
And his people continue
To watch for Falling Rock.

II

Farm Tales

Home in the Still Hours

At times I feel the smallness of my life
Here on these few acres
Where I have everything I need:
Good dirt to plant in,
Space to be alone and my tribe nearby,
An open view to the mountains,
A peaceful sky above,
Deep, deep roots that feed me,
And ghosts I know and love.

Honor Among Trees

> *"Every leaf seems to speak."*
> — John Muir

I put my faith in these trees.
I find the strength to grow on
in the trees I have planted,
when I remember to learn
what they teach.

The big maple, the silver patron
saint, protector, and old friend,
shows me the true meaning
of shelter.

And this exuberant little apple tree
decked out in blossoms so heavy
branches are completely obscured
in a cloak of a thousand promises.
Every bit of good in the world
began as a good intention,
a promise from the heart.

Now I see these young aspens
have grown into a grove, a colony;
the family's first new trunk today
is knee-high and thriving.
Brand new leaves shimmer
in a sunlit breeze and kindle
my hope for tomorrow.

I do find my faith in the trees on this land
where I am rooted as deeply as these
trees I have nurtured,
the trees that I love.
Every leaf does speak.

Angus in Late Winter

New neighbors have taken up residence
in the pasture east of the house,
where—for the past 25 years or so—
horses, bred and trained for dressage,
characterized the space.
There is nothing French about these
new unhurried souls, moving
heavily and sturdily—
rootedness in motion—
their solid black bodies plodding
silhouettes against a patchy
snow and grass mosaic.

2021 Apologizes with a Gift

It could not have had a more mundane start,
this last morning of a brutal year,
a day when many others are readying
a celebration, chilling champagne
for a gathering of friends,
I choose instead to clean my house,
clear some clutter,
sweep the floors,
do the laundry.
Just as I drop a basket of dirty clothes
beside the washing machine,
the most spectacular murmuration of starlings
swoops past the back window,
blackening it, actually blocking
the light coming through for a second.
I rush to the window.   There must be
five hundred birds—more! more!—
on the ground, like a black pool
in the pasture south of the house.
        Jack! Jack! Come see! I call out
and the starlings swoop up, up
into the two big cottonwoods by the field gate,
the winter-bare trees blackened now by bird bodies.
I open the back door to listen—their screeching sound,
a true cacophony fills the Jerome Prairie air.

> *I want to make them fly*, I say
and slam the door. A small group,
as if on an elastic tether, flies out and back
to the clamoring tree.
I slam the door again and whoop out a holler, too.
The cottonwoods explode
in sudden motion, a black mass
swirls out, curves around, ripples
like a rapid in a sky river,
then slacks like a cut-bank eddy—
synchronized swimmers swooping, swooping—
then vanishing into the morning fog.
> *I hope they come back.*
I'd very much like to see that again,
to lose my breath and beating heart
to the beauty of a thousand wings.

Divine Trinity

Come March, my fingers itch and I can't wait
to share in the miracle of the seed.
In early Spring-like days, my hopes inflate.
Greens and sweet peas assuage my pent-up need,
and gladly I fall on my knees to weed
in the company of frogs, still inert.
I rise and wipe soiled hands on my shirt,
see pear trees confess their first signs of bud.
Divine Trinity: water, sun and dirt.
In March, life bursts forth, swelling to a flood.

Pi Day, from the front porch

Perfect slice of Pi
Day: sunlight tatted into
Pink lace plum blossoms

3.14.2018

Secrets in the Garden

You know it's time to get started
When a whole fistful of dirt
Crumbles free through your open fingers.
The sting of a bitter winter eases
In the warming, drying ground.

Plant them deep, if depth is needed
(Some are fine just barely covered)
And don't worry — it's really second nature.
We all reap exactly what we sow.
Don't plant all you have all at once.

It won't take long for green to show
Above in leaf; below the roots
Of secrets that have tapped your heart
For more seasons than we can count
Are deep, going deeper underground.

What April Brings

Honeybees are turning blossoms into pears,
a magic trick only they can perform.

Song sparrows making love on the morning porch
will soon fill the bird boxes with new singers.

Little grape hyacinths popping up all over
are sweet surprises scattered by garden gnomes.

In the South pasture, a new-born calf
is licked to its feet,
totters twice from mother's tongue
and is wholly right in the world.

Here we are in another April
of pandemic-lockdown-woe
feeling as if life has ended,
a grim assessment,
a morbid hyperbole refuted
by a glance in any direction.

To April, who dallied

The daffodils are past full bloom, already
browning at the frilly edges, having been
battered by hailstones and rain squalls,
drooped by hard frosts
at the end of a lion March.

Your late arrival is most
welcome. Relief comes at last,

for now blossoms swell
to bursting on the pear trees,
hyacinths bloom as a grounded rainbow,
columbine buds rise on proud stems,
forsythia makes bright noise from the back row
with the flowering plum and bridal wreath

and everywhere there is
new green,
shocks of yellow,
splashes of pink.

Oh April,
Your cruelty is your indolent pace,
Beauty your redemption.

Monday

The sun burned off the fog fairly early
to cast new light on a fair morning

Pear trees in full blossom
are off to another good start

And the pasture green-up is
almost too keen to take in

All is coming on
to begin again

New leaf, upstart grass
nest-building sparrows, opening flowers

In a palette so vivid, to take more
than a sweeping glance is to be

overcome by a burgeoning spring
and swallowed whole by April

In the garden

this afternoon, I closed my eyes
to contemplate a nap and the last page
I read in the book still open
across my bookshelf lap
and I heard a coming wind—
water running through April cottonwoods—
I heard it approaching from the south
coming over the Siskiyous and down
the north face of Marble Mountain
Long before I was rustled enough
to look as well as listen
I heard the wind heading my way—
a murmuration of winged ghosts

Mimic

"Learn to see—Everything is connected to everything else."
— Leonardo Da Vinci

I heard the red-shouldered hawk
and quickly looked up, trying
to catch him in flight,
scanned the sky above the pond,
and the trees the hawk likes,
when again the hawk calls
      'kee-yeeear, kee-yeeear'
and the song sparrow nesting
in the house on the big maple
startles to def-con three status,
two frogs dive, catching the attention
of the old barn cat, Tux,
when a blue jay swoops in
to land on the bench
on the back deck
and lets out, clear and true
      'kee-yeeear, kee-yeeear.'

A Good Day

We go walking, and so often
You take my hand. It feels right.
The world settles down. No noise
Only birdsong and a breezy rustle
In newly unfurled cottonwood leaves.
With a startling rush, the neighbor's dog
Runs the feeding Canada Geese
In Tom's field, lifts the flock to flight
And I can hear the weight of reluctance
In the heavy beat of wings.
We watch together as the geese
Rise on impossible wings and clamoring air,
Sounding their grievance across the open prairie.
Your warm hand tightens slightly around mine
And having come to the end of our road,
My hand in yours, we amble home.

Persephone

Sunlight hangs in raindrops poised to fall
from fading plum blossoms, sparkling gems
fracturing the cleanest light we have seen in months.

Full-spectrum hope arcs above the emerald pastures
and forces recall of an innocence
we can no longer claim nor cherish.

All the promise in April's pastel flourish
is but a brief hour in passing,
a covenant breached in its making

soon will turn to garish summer,
be burned to ash by brazen autumn,
and in winter, interred with corpses.

In the Garden, Early

These hands are a blessing,
I think, as I loosen the hilled soil
to coax a few new potatoes,
little creamers from the earth,
my fingers blindly teasing
the small tubers free,
leaving the stones and clods behind,
under this wide-open sky,
the only sound my shallow breath
and ungloved sifting.

Still Life with Heron

At first glance, unseen
(such stillness can be missed)
until some silent fish,
a feeding trout, perhaps, dimples
the surface of the still water
just above the mouth of
Slate Creek, and the heron
turns his steady gaze one tick
to the west. Here where the air
tastes of big leaf maple
and smells of slow river,
the heron measures
the way of the trout
and returns to stillness again.

Laying to Rest on the Farm
for E. Norma Skitty, with love

With the sober deliberateness
of a military funeral, she carries
the small body, wrapped in a soft piece
torn from a worn-out linen shirt
to the west side of the pond.
In the shade of young aspens
the soft ground yields easily
under the shovel head. Startled
by how quickly the Earth opens
like the door of an old friend
giving overdue welcome and greeting
to a long-missed fellow
she deliberately slows her work,
not wanting to rush this farewell
to a loyal companion, who
for eighteen years brought love
to a house filled with
unrelenting silences
undesired solitude
unacknowledged grief.

Night Sky

To see the moon
In the company of stars
Gives me hope

They are nothing alike
Don't even come from the same
Neighborhood—not even close—

But there they are
Right up there
Hanging together

Shining the same light
In different ways
Each one made more beautiful

By the company of another
The light of the better world
More beautiful together

III

Farm-Grown Theology

One World

> *"a leaf of grass is no less than*
> *the journey-work of the stars."*
> Walt Whitman, *Song of Myself*

It is all one and none
as splendid without the other.
Where does the beauty of the leaf end
and the tree begin? or the tree end
and the forest begin? How does one
distinguish the fragrant marvel of the forest
from the astounding grandeur of the mountains?
or the shaded river pool
where the water slows to cool
as separate from the rapid run
to a plunging waterfall?
A flower, a frog, a hawk in the sky,
a fir cone, a sparrow, a blackberry vine,
salmon and weasel and humankind,
We are all one and none
lives well, none lives long alone.

Theology

"Every natural object is a conductor of divinity."
— John Muir

With roots growing deep and branches sky-high
the divinity of trees in inarguable;
so too a red-shouldered hawk in miraculous flight
and the fruits of autumn in bright April blooms.

The divinity of trees is a plainsong for all
giving thanks to soil and water and worms
and the fruits of autumn now in the blossoms:
sacred offspring of sunlight and hope.

Thanks to the soil and water and worms.
Tender thanks to the Earth for all that is holy,
Every child of sunlight and unfettered hope,
honor our mother, our cradle and dreams.

Give praise for the Earth for all that is holy,
send it aloft with a hawk in free flight;
honor our home, our floor and our roof.
Roots grow ever deeper and dreams reach the sky.

Gaia

So much of the goodness here on Earth
seems like gifts from the Goddess,
unexpected presents of joy,
some tucked here and there,
like the first crocus to show
its bright color, poking through
a melting crust of snow,
and some more showy delights—
the apple trees covered
in pink and white blossoms,
promising a great bounty
to be delivered in autumn.
Summer's best gifts might be
those that arrive by air mail—
the impossibly bright colors
of tanagers in the pines,
or the clear sailing song
of Western Meadowlarks.
Also pleasures at ground-level—
an abundance of berries
and honeybee hum,
tree-shaded refuge
from a hot sun,
wind in the field grass,
a killdeer's fine acting,
a river that runs
from slow water to rapids,
and here and there, falls.
Give thanks and much gratitude
to our mother, our Earth,
generous, lovely and rich.

Optimism: Late January

This Oregon winter rain
Washes the old
Stubborn leaves down,
Washes gray
Branches clean.
Stripped bare,
They reach higher,
Spread wider,
Open to newness
When it comes.
Falling straight down,
Falling hard,
Earnest, serious rain
Splashes up some
Piece of history.
Blurs the eyes,
Clears the perspective,
Winter rain coming down,
Smelling like forgiveness.

Sunday

A warm April morning
under a flawless blue sky
has the song sparrows singing
of nesting their young
between home deliveries
of moss and shed feathers,
in flight after flutter,
uplifted and prompted
by these lengthening days.

My morning unfolds gently
without a single anxious note.
There is time for birds today,
time for nests of gathered goods.
Today there is time for these wings.

Pocket Full of Springtime

Trees are sky farmers
harvesting sunlight and air
fresh enough to breathe

4.20

Columbine in bloom:
beauty of complexity
rooted in our grief.

Wild Connotations

Wilderness is not
the antonym of Heaven:
this thesaurus lies.

Earth Day

Planting a new tree
is a prayer for a future
where everyone breathes.

The Peace of These Waters
      — beside the Middle Rogue

Forever arriving and leaving,
perpetually present, never absent,
time doesn't stop but it surely dallies,
here on the bank of the Middle Rogue.

I come down to the river
to let go of regrets and heartaches,
to send ghosts and demons downstream,
let them move away and out to sea.

And I come to the river
to ponder what is coming my way,
to consider the drift of new currents
and the wash of fresh opportunity;
looking upriver, squinting in the glinting
light on riffled water, I can see
sometimes what might be possible.

And here by the river, I can stay
still, unhurried; nothing makes demands
on my time and attention
except a pair of red-tail hawks
in flight, too beautiful to ignore.

Holy Water, Holy Ground
—*in praise of the North Fork Malheur*

Birdsong and the river laughing
as it tumbles and gurgles
over a pebbled bed so rich in color
an Earthborne rainbow winks
from the creek bottom; above
sunlight twinkles as faceted stones
in living water, holy water.
Wild geraniums bloom pink
alongside the deer path to the river
and at the feet of the forest Elders,
these yellow-bellied Ponderosas,
devout throngs of purple lupine and lily,
columbine and meadow-foam.
A light wind moves silently, gently
through the trees, giving just a sway,
a graceful waltz. ——Then out of the blue
—— a tanager flashes ——
impossibly bright —— yellow streak
against dark evergreens. Now orange
butterfly, orange butterflies and again
the plainsong of the birds
and the running water
of a high-mountain trout stream.
All that is holy,
all that's divine is here
in this cathedral of light.

High Desert Gospel

I will not live my life for a metaphor,
Rather find divinity in blackberry clouds
Hung like royal birthday bunting
Over the high desert. This austere Eden
Desiccates and filets faith in anything
more transcendent than wind and dust,
Anything more abstract than sagebrush.
Look across spare distances and light
Delivers in shimmers, like mercury loosed.
Look across to a mile-wide plank
Of steel rain vanishing in the desert air.

Sound is mute, color subliminal.
Postulate life and wait: affirmation comes
From a stir in the cheat grass,
A shadow in flight, the distant rumble
Of horses descending an ancient wash.

This place is mother to nothing
But time, borne out in the gnarled junipers,
Witnessed in the symbiosis
Of want and satisfaction as a single frame of mind.
A density of memory is the lone excess:
Petroglyphs, trail ruts, range fire chars—
Recollections spanning ten-thousand years
Occupy the same present and leave
Still open space for a high desert miracle:
        A singular sense of self,
            Knowing the terrible smallness of one.
It's a slow climb to a stone
Lesson of the will.   Low
Thunder gives it voice.

In August

Somewhere a band is playing
            —a marching tune
            or perhaps a dirge—
carried in on breathless air
now rattling parched August leaves
            one against another

The long day begins to close down

Here a tin bucket weeps its load
on cracked cement and still
the garish sun refuses to go down,
            —a needling presence
            a straw man with a witless tongue—

Nowhere is the sky more oppressive
in its scale, pressed and stretched
above the bone-dry prairie
            —how easily we can lose
            our way on homeland soil—
ground too hard to give or yield

The way is one of six directions
but it's nowhere on this map
            —squinting hard against our tears
            and still we cannot see it—
blinded as we are by the dry
eye-numbing light of August

October Disclaimer

I found myself in the library.
My notions were scattered like leaves
that had been raked and piled
and dived into by a pack of
soft-soled 10-year-olds on sugar.
You know what they can do.
I own too many books.
You can see there are more than I can hold.
I carry them wherever I go.
Collected leaves.

Deliverance

In July when the world caught fire,
whole forests moved into the air,
a vaporized Birnam Wood.

Next year we hope for
torrents of mercy from bulging storm clouds
out of a Turner painting.

When we hear again
the clement sound of heavy rain,
like a drum line pushing a marching band,

We will lift our children onto our shoulders
to see better what they feel coming,
to taste the cool water of deliverance.

Where We Stand
for Dad in his centennial year

I think of you always as standing
on the far shore of Babyfoot Lake,
where the treeline and shoreline were once
one and the same, evergreen and light

before the big fires—
Silver, Biscuit, Chetco, Klondike—
burned through and through again,
burned hot and hotter still

the forest stands still, bearing charred witness
with two hillsides of black and ashy skeletons,
a cemetery of silhouetted crosses
haunting the lake with these reflected ghosts

yet I recall you standing just there—
the heel of the lake between us—
the water both reflecting the light
and swallowing it whole

into the deep, it disappears, only glinting
a little in the shallows of the lapping shore.
What craft might close the span between us
or this memory of trees and light?

Morning in Fire Season

The sparrows were singing
in the first blue-sky morning
after weeks of longing for a clean breath.
The sparrows were singing
when the sun started its climb
and the smoke its daily descent
into the river valley, obscuring
the mountains where it grew.
The sparrows were still singing
when a raucous flock
of Canada geese emerged
out of the thickening smoke,
like winged apparitions, anguished
souls taking shadowy form.
Still the sparrows were singing
when the red-tail came in low
under a browning sky
to perch on the fence post
behind the big maple,
and the sparrows' song went still.

Fire Season 2022:
To August, in the hottest year now on record

As this brutal season begins
to come to its end,
begins to wind down to something kinder,
the scent of Autumn a hint in the morning air,
our eyes stay focused on the near horizon,
looking for signs warning us
this summer will not go
quietly into its goodnight.

What new heartache might you bring?
What more sacrifice will you demand?
Another hundred-thousand trees?
Salmon belly-up in a hot river,
muddied, reddened and fouled?
Perhaps the silencing of frogs,
or the growing absence of birdsong?
In truth, the penance should be ours,
as is the sin, the blame,
the crying shame.

Oh, August, will you exact a full reckoning
and without mercy
take the forests,
chum the waters,
choke the breath from the sky?
Oh, ash will fall on the butterfly's wings
and even song sparrows
won't sing.

Fire Season 2022: The Rum Creek burn

Ash falls on all, even
a late-summer rose's bright pink
is muted and speckled
by blackened remains from ten billion
burnt fir needles
and shapeless gray bits
of madrone bark,
oak leaf,
whirligig maple seed—
all and more carried up, up
on towering plumes, up
into high winds fueled by rising heat—
drift for miles and fall
enriching only the dirt.

We all—every living thing—all
are born of the Earth
and in death, returned to the Earth,
throughout life, fed by the Earth
and sheltered.

This late-August wildfire
makes plain the old words:
ashes to ashes and
dust to dust.
The cycle goes 'round.
A circle completes itself,
and the wind bellows and blows.

Only the dirt prospers.
Only the dirt gains ground.

Blackberry Eating in 2022, our hottest year yet on record
after Galway Kinnell

Scrounge up a few with a little juice,
and mostly get nothing more
than scratched and purpled hands.
Oh, *the fat, overripe, icy, black blackberries*
have this year been scorched and shrunk
into shriveled berry carcasses,
tiny black carbuncles so decrepit
even a chough takes no interest,
nor a mourning dove,
nor a skunk.
They were overripe jam-on-the-vine
before they had a chance to get fat,
before they took the shape of those
many-lettered, one-syllabled lumps.
Two strangling heat-domes were two too many,
and six parched months in a row—
all the Spring and all the Summer—
turned late September blackberry eating
to a prickly old memory,
now fossilized on a moribund Earth
and bitter on my dusty tongue.

Mercy, Mercy
after Marvin Gaye

Consumers and travelers, please have some mercy.
Hikers and campers, we must show her mercy.
Our planet, our home, will die from our me, me, me, me!

What is the value of madly acquiring more material things,
or traipsing the world just to be where we ain't?
We move. We camp. We move again. Then what?

We cannot point fingers and blame them and they,
as we build fetid mountains, casting off all we have used,
fouling the Earth until there's no home to go home to.

Is this what we want the future to be?
Our children left with who-knows-what,
surviving by picking in garbage and slogging about

in poisonous ooze? What kind of living is this?
Open space gone, smallest towns overcrowded,
cities sprawl outward and smother the land.

We know what to do and we even know how.
Still the tyranny of greed and wanting too much
impoverishes all and gives nothing more.

We must stop all this planetary abuse.
Earth's where we are, not where we are from.
Give her your Love, every woman and man.

Live free of harm! We must urgently do all we can
to prevent our mother's dreadful demise. She
is Life. She is Life! Mercy, mercy, we must take a stand.

Not with a Bang, but a Whimper

The dissolution of the planet came
much earlier than we planned on,
too late to make our stand on
the veracity of replicated science,
the wisdom of dedicated lives.
We never imagined the sound
of the planet dying would soothe
our accumulated fears,
would bathe our ears
in tender strains;
not Beethoven banging at the beast,
not frantic Mozart racing
to outpace the inward collapse;
it is the lullaby we so desire,
the resting, at last, alone in the cradle
rocking us into our watery graves.
We fall here now,
not with a dirge
but a muted hallelujah
farewell.

The Pagan Prays Under a Dry Sky

Leaves from the big maple fall
uncertainly, dried to weightlessness
in arid frozen air, so lacking in humidity
no frost formed at 29 degrees.
Whisper of light, light wind rattles
these dried bones of clattering
leaves and sets them loose in the wild
flurries of Autumn. November now
and still no rain in sight.

Fears of another dry winter,
another year of unrelenting drought,
long seasons of nursing
the farm, the garden, the trees
on tears and well-water from a hose,
metering it out for survival,
having given up on thriving long ago.
The death of each planted life is a loss
we cannot recover. No bells will toll
for these long-limbed beloved souls.

Mulch the leaves.
Clean the neighbor's chicken coop
for the composting litter.
Feed the garden soil.
Nurse the trees with love.
Believe in the power of the Pacific.
Believe the rains will come.
The rains will come.

The World is Mud-luscious

For the first time in far too long,
the ground is thoroughly soaked,
the mud is deep and beautiful.
The pond is full.
Rainwater is pooled in the pastures,
and drips from the refreshed trees
dressed in glossy new leaves,
their branches reach out and up,
like true believers exalting their god.

So grateful for the dark grey skies,
for the pregnant clouds delivering life-
sustaining rain, so thankful
for reason to think
this drought may end,
the trees may thrive,
the Earth may start to heal,
my eyes need not see the stars
to fill my heart with dreams.

To my future grandchildren

I pin my hopes on the power
of Natural Selection, that
the environment of the future
favors the kind and the gentle,
that Mother Nature, in her need,
nurtures and chooses the genes
for intelligence and honor, that
those who strive to protect the planet,
our home, will survive
the ravages of this climate crisis—
the fires and floods,
the toxic air and water—
will rise above the outbreaks
of ignorance and hatred and greed, these
diseases of the heart and mind,
the body and breath, that
have pushed our Mother to the edge,
to the tipping point on the last step
at Death's door.
I have to believe
the future will belong to you
who strive to heal and preserve,
who learn and understand,
adapt and evolve
as mother-loving Earthlings.

IV

Here and There

This Flight Cannot be Cancelled

"Wanna fly you got to give up the shit that weighs you down."
— Toni Morrison

> So we begin again
> on another trip around the sun,
> starting here, starting now
> in these shortest days,
> the darkest hours lit by hope alone,
> looking toward the shine,
> yearning for the season of light
> when sunflowers sing their hymns,
> faces turned and turning to follow
> the god they worship.

We must turn, too, and sing with hope.
After two full years of near constant Decembering,
those countless days of missing and remembering
must now yield. Out of reach just a week ago,
that which seemed absurdly rose-colored
is now perched atop an easy upslope as we fly
into tomorrow, resolute, inspired, encouraged.

> A new year has come, caroling with blue-sky brightness,
> it's time to set down yesterday's weight;
> it's time to set an interesting course
> over this yet untravelled way,
> and soar, unburdened,
> through this wide and variable sky.

Here, where I write, I have much:
an open view across the valley
to mountains rising in the west;
space enough for solitude
but no yawing loneliness.   Birds
sheltering in place know
silence is a kind of safety,
wordless company, a comfort.

> I know.
> It's time to go.
> It's time now to go.
> Tip a glass. Take a breath.
> Let it go.

My Perennial Love

Every year when the spring bulbs'
show is done, stems bereft of bloom,
my lust for color is satisfied next
by a brilliant succession of bursting
red and pink and purple and white
on the woody stemmed and evergreen
perennials, the reliable journeymen
of the garden. They never disappoint.
By June, the summer annuals catch
my wandering eye. They flirt and charm
and I always bring some home,
well-aware that they are flashes-
in-the-pan and pots, beautiful
and irresistible. These courtships
do not last long—a few months at most.
They need a lot of attention,
never make it through the tough times,
and rarely come back on their own.
My heart belongs to the steady, the dependable
rhodies, camelias, daphne, azaleas,
columbine, lupine, mock orange, and phlox,
lilacs, lavender, primroses and roses.
Such trusty, well-grounded troopers,
constant and generous. Loyal.
They stand the tests of time,
like you, my perennial love.
Like you.

Life is not like the movies

particularly the ending
which rarely comes cleanly,
sublimely, or with high drama,
no unexpected turn and tragic end
to a high-speed chase
in pursuit of some
hatched golden egg

mostly, we end quietly,
succumbing to our life-
long lousy habits
and poor choices.

mostly we go off
stage left, into the darkness
of an unremarkable gloaming
never having been
a star, we exit

without a guiding light
without a guardian angel
without a farewell scene
or a loving hand
gentling our fears

without words of kind reassurance
or remembrance
mostly we end in silence

mostly we end alone

Becoming Homeless
> "Home is the place where, when you have to go there,
> they have to take you in."
> — Robert Frost in *The Death of the Hired Man*

The old house on the hilltop sold quickly,
was emptied and scrubbed clean,
no trace of us left behind,
(except the laundry room door-jamb,
measuring stick for two-and-a-half generations.)

Closing and locking up for the last time
felt like another death in the family.
"We're really orphans now," I said to my sisters.
The oldest shot me a steely-eyed wordless scold.
The closest, tearing up, said,*"Don't make me cry."*
Then our youngest brother called everyone together;
"Let's get a picture," and we all lined up
on the front walk by the locked door.
"No rabbit ears!" teased our other brother,
resurrecting Mom's family-photo mantra
and prompting laughs. *"Get ready!"*
The camera's timer flashed its countdown
and we all put on our *Cheeeese*-smiles.

The picture turned out alright, there are a few
rabbit ears and the smiles look real.
But I see that as a picture of mourners.
I see us all as newly homeless orphans.

A house is emptied and sold,
memories saved in photos,
artifacts sorted and kept.
But the home that was is gone forever.
We can no longer go there;
they will not take us in.
A house is sold.
A home is lost.

Extraterrestrial Plain

Looks to me like the surface of Mars,
and it is marked, it seems,
with crop circles and seams,
like it's been visited
by the same visitors
we have hosted,
those who left
unnatural impressions
on the good people
of Iowa and Kansas
and other flat places
that naturally offer up
vast amber fields of grain
good for mashing, good
for Earth-borne art and signage
pressed into service
to distinguish the dreamers
and believers
from the skeptics
who put borders and limits
on all sorts of things,
like imagination
and wonder,
who look at the night sky
and see only lonely rocks
adrift in the cosmic stream,
see not the light
but the darkness between.

Directive for an uprooted soul
found poem drawn from
The Peregrine, by J.A. Baker

You must
travel like birds;
fears and fields
hide the tremor
of the still tree
across open ground.
Grow.
Be alone.
Learn to become
an arrow, a tree.
Yesterday is a week ago.
Endure.

John Muir in Big Pines

At the Big Pines R.V. Park,
as a wet mid-April blow is coming in,
wilderness seekers watch their big-screen TVs
inside aluminum and vinyl boxes
lit up like Macy's holiday windows,
and I think of a man, so in love
with trees, he belts himself
into the forest canopy to know
how trees feel in the wild
Pacific storms — Odysseus on the mast
listening in agony for the Sirens' song.

Me Tarzan. You Cheeta?

Cheeta died in Palm Harbor, Florida,
Christmas Eve 2011.
Kidney failure. Once his obituary
was in the paper, heartfelt words
of grief and condolences came
in cards and letters from around the world,
and several edible bouquets made of fruit,
all addressed to the deceased
in care of his captors
at the Suncoast Primate Sanctuary.
Mourners wrote of years long ago—
          thanks for the memories, several of them said—
and fondly recalled times spent
with this friend, now dearly departed.

So marks the end of a long-running,
fairly profitable con.
Cheeta of Palm Harbor was a good draw;
pitched as an endearing character
with a silver screen backstory,
he was the marquee fundraiser for Suncoast.
But Palm Harbor Cheeta wasn't in the movies,
he wasn't 80 years old as claimed
(twice the average lifespan of a captive),
he wasn't comic relief.
          He was taken as a child from his family.
          He was sold and resold
          into a lifetime of servitude.
          He was worked,
          exploited to profit others,
          kept for years in near
          solitary confinement,
          deprived of a natural life.
          Deprived of his nature.
          But thousands of Floridian tourists
          wanted to believe
          in his Hollywood past
          and thought he was cute in a hat.

After Reading Ray Carver's *Egress*

"What the hell? Who needs
death or notebooks?" he asked
and I thought, That's right.
Both are insidious pits —
my house is littered
with used-up and half-dead
notebooks and tablets
scratch pads and pages—
they are everywhere, haunting me
like unclaimed corpses in the morgue,
fallen soldiers still on the field.

There's a kind of death for words
that never drew a good breath,
never lived inside a cogent line.

School Crossing

It was September back-to-school for 3rd grade
when Andy got his store-bought eye-patch;
it was black, sort of shiny,
and we were all real happy for him.

For weeks, every recess we played
a new game on the merry-go-round and monkey bars.
We called it Pirate Ship.
Andy was always Captain.

The fun lasted through most of October
until discussion of Halloween costumes
crept into our Pirate Ship talk,
and Brandon, the new kid from California,
said he was *going to be Andy for Halloween,*
said his mom already bought him his *own eye patch.*

Time stopped.   We all glared at Brandon
then looked up at Andy as he came down
from the ship's wheelhouse atop the monkey bars
to trudge, head-down, toward our classroom door.

Why'd you go and say that!? Barry yelled.
Yeah, Brand-dumb, Mattie added. *You jerk!*
Denny punched him in the nose, drew blood.
Carla whacked his legs with her swashbuckling stick,
made his eyes water and cringe.
We all turned on him and followed Andy in.

The new kid didn't know, like we all did,
how Andy lost his left eye in 1st grade
when his dad got real drunk
and poked Andy's eye out with a fork.
His dad went to jail and never came back.

Through the rest of first grade, Andy's eye
was covered with taped-on gauze.
There was no hope of saving his sight.
In 2nd grade he wore a homemade eye-patch
his mom sewed up with denim
cut from out-grown jeans.

So 3rd grade Pirate Ship games abruptly ended.
By spring, we were making water guns
with latex tubing and ball-point pen parts.
Brandumb was regularly hosed.

A couple of years later, Andy's mom remarried
and Andy got fitted with a glass eye.
Sometimes he'd bring his spare to school
and just for laughs, he'd put the eye on his tongue,
and open his mouth wide in Brandumb's face.

Arlen Furst Walks Past His Wife

People go nuts every day.
Not in spectacular, news-making ways,
Most step anonymously across the line
Into lengthening silences and
Private disappointments.

Men past forty
Women past sixty
Plodding through their lives
Deluded by their own pretenses
Of meaning.

Arlen Furst walks past his hand-wringing wife
And opens the holding pen gate
Bulging now against the moving mass
Of white-faced calves.
Riding the back-swinging gate, he whistles.
There's tangible fear in the herd,
Heads held unnaturally high and turned,
Eyes crazed back, wide whites, panicked.
The herd, pushing through the steel gate,
Moves as a single entity.
Waves of motion roll across the brown backs.

In mid-winter
Before the first glut,
He'd sorted and sold
The bigger calves.
But it wasn't enough.
It is never enough.

Birds fell from the sky like tears

Fierce winds out of Africa whipped
north across the Mediterranean,
a swift sword cutting
through the great Aegean flyway,
creating impossible tailwinds
for thousands of swifts and swallows
in seasonal migration.
The head-on collision with cross-
winds off the continent,
an exhaled breath of betrayal,
knocked the migrants down
and out of flight. Birds fell
from the sky like tears
from an anguished God,
fell into the turquoise sea, countless in number,
fell by the thousands on island towns and gardens,
hundreds on the beach by Homer's rock,
dozens on the grounds of Nea Moni
where the arrest of Jesus
is enshrined in Byzantine mosaic.

Aberrant October

Some curated collection of memories
is all that remains,
and an ill-defined longing
for the familiar,
for the old ways,
for the old world,
old rhythms and old friends.

In 207 days of Corona cloistering
the world has gone under
an alien transformation,
has undergone an unholy
transfiguration. Faith is
burned, blown and diseased.

I find myself picking up and saving
little treasures as I wander the farm,
a collection of offerings—
snail shell, blue feather, speckled rock—

and I glean the last garden produce,
noticing long shadows
in ever shorter days.

The Fall

A week ago, the big maple glowed,
radiating yellow light, electrified,
made golden by autumn sunlight.
Such beauty never lasts.
Today nearly bare branches
reach across a burdened sky,
gray and ghostly in the morning fog.
Beauty cannot survive in this world—
wind, rain, bluster, blow and away it goes.

Everything falls. Leaves, rain, warmth, light—
spirits driven down on worn out knees,
weak and creaking, too sore for honest prayer.
Let it be. Fall, fall, let it all come down
on to fallow fields, on to fevered ground.
Let these days be masked and smothered
by the foul breath of corruption,
the Earth pock-marked with graves
for five million tainted corpses.

Near the end of a hard climb

Leg muscles burning and just
a few more ways to try,
the instinct is to put your head down
and grind out the final
uphill push—
to prioritize finishing
over experiencing—
destination over
journey—
but nearing the end
of a hard climb is the time
to keep your head up—
to look out over the forest canopy
reaching up from the canyon below,
to notice the ribbon of river
glinting in winks and shimmies,
to breathe clean air rinsed
in sun-warmed cedar and fir—
and take your time;
the top of this tough hill is just
a few more steps ahead.

Lightfall

Up early on this uncertain Sunday,
a dim pre-dawn half-light hangs
over the still sleeping pastures.
Then in the west, unexpected brightness
shines the crest of Page Mountain
out and beyond the nearest hills,
above a river of morning fog.
The beauty catches my breath.

A new day comes,
not all at once to all—
look up and out, look ahead and beyond
to the places touched by earliest light,
to where the light falls first.
Every day begins in darkness
that will not go on;
every darkness finally yields
to a breaking dawn.

The Elk in Spring

We saw the elk today,
Driving home on I-5 southbound
And there they were
In the meadow just
West of the freeway
Near milepost 82.
We've seen them here before,
A magnificent herd —
Roosevelt elk, 20 or more —
The simple fact of them, easily
Grazing on someone's back 40,
Maybe 60 yards off the interstate
Is a rose-colored miracle:
        One moment to believe that
        Our damage can be undone,
        That things will be alright.

Acknowledgements

Thanks to the editors of these publications where several of the poems in *Jerome Prairie Creation Myths and other Farm Tales* previously appeared.

Encore Prize Poems 2018 *Laying to Rest on the Farm* (National Federation of State Poetry Societies, 2018)

Encore Prize Poems 2018 *Where We Stand* (National Federation of State Poetry Societies, 2020)

From the Heart of the Applegate *High Desert Gospel* (Applegate Valley Community Newspaper, Inc., 2016)

Penned Up: Writing Out the Pandemic *Holy Solstice* (Applegate Poets and N8tive Run Press, 2021)

The Applegater, Winter 2020. *Late Summer Field Guide* (Applegate Valley Community Newspaper, Vol.15, No.2)

The Applegater, Summer 2022.*One World* (Applegate Valley Community Newspaper, Vol.15, No.2)

Gratitudes

With gratitude, thanks go out to all my family and friends.

I also am grateful for the support from my wonderful Applegate
Poets and for the new energy from the fabulous Perigee Poets.

My heart overflows with gratitude and admiration for my son.

Bent Sonnet for Nick

Standing here before me, you're a gift,
Open-hearted, smiling, glad to be alive,
No longer slave to debilitating genes,
Nor pounded down by self-inflicted pain,
Each day you greet now as a treasured friend who
Time and trust brought to your door.
Forget the terrors of time gone by,
Out, out with self-harm and loathing.
Remember a human's stay on Earth is finite and brief;
Make yours count, make it rich and sweet.
You can never know just how a life will
Bend and curve until it does, and then
On you go, on you go, and know
You are loved as you are. You are so loved.

About the Poet

Lisa E Baldwin, a fifth-generation rural Oregonian, has lived in the Lower Applegate Valley since 1966. After teaching English for 30 years, she retired in 2015 and began her current career as a Poetry Evangelist—writing and publishing poetry, organizing and teaching poetry workshops, spreading the good news of the poetry world, and encouraging others to write as an act of art. Baldwin created and facilitated the 2018 *Poetry Alive!* workshops and *Something About Poetry 2019* and *2021* seminars for the Josephine Community Library which are resuming, post-pandemic, in April 2023. She is past-president of the Oregon Poetry Association and a long-time chair of the statewide *Cascadia* Contest for Oregon's K-12 students, and currently serves as an OPA liaison for the Oregon Poetry Collection housed in the Knight Library at the University of Oregon. She also serves on the Board of Directors and the writing team for the Applegate Valley Community Newsmagazine. Baldwin's poetry has appeared in the *Jefferson Journal, Crosswinds Poetry Journal, WomanChrist: 30th Anniversary Edition, The Applegater, Grants Pass Daily Courier,* several issues of *Verseweavers,* the *Encore Prize Poems 2020* and *2018,* and regional anthologies */pãn | dé | mïk / 2020, From the Heart of the Applegate, Moments Before Midnight, Penned Up: Writing Out the Pandemic,* and *Reading the River.* Baldwin's first book of poetry, *Truths and Consequences,* was published in 2021.